Dismissing Problem Employees

By Daniel Barnett

The Employment Law Library

All books in the Employment Law Library are sent for free to members of the HR Inner Circle.

Published by Employment Law Services Limited, Unit 3, Chequers Farm, Chequers Lane, Watford, Hertfordshire WD25 0LG

ISBN 978-1-913925-17-8

Acknowledgments

Welcome to book 19 in this series of mini guides on employment law for HR professionals.

My main thanks go to Liesel Bullas for her help with the first draft of this book.

None of these books are possible without the input and experience of the members of the HR Inner Circle. I write these small books for you, and you get them for free as part of your membership.

Many of the ideas in this book were drawn from members' experiences and questions in our online community and on our Q&A calls. James Fairchild, Penelope Douglass, Micky Marsden, Jane Rawlins and Julie Barter, all of whom are members of the HR Inner Circle, commented on the manuscript and offered suggestions to improve it.

Thanks also to Susan Keillor and Josh Powell for beta-reading the manuscript, Tincuta Collett for the layout and design, Aaron Gaff for proofreading and Maria Rodriguez for converting the book into the formats needed for Amazon.

If you're not a member of the HR Inner Circle and you're interested in learning more about HR Inner Circle membership (www.hrinnercircle.co.uk), there is some information at the back of this book.

Daniel Barnett
June 2024

ABOUT THE AUTHOR

Daniel Barnett is a leading employment law barrister practising from Outer Temple Chambers. With 25 years' experience defending public and private sector employers against employment claims, he has represented a Royal Family, several international airlines, FTSE-100 companies and various NHS Trusts and local authorities. Employee clients include David & Victoria Beckham's nanny and Paul Mason (subject of the ITV documentary 'Britain's Fattest Man').

Daniel is a past chair of the Employment Lawyers' Association's publishing committee and electronic services working party. He is the author or co-author of eight books, including the Law Society Handbook on Employment Law (currently in its 8th edition). He is the creator of the Employment Law (UK) mailing list, an email alerter bulletin service sending details of breaking news in employment law three times a week to 33,000 recipients.

Legal directories describe him as 'extremely knowledgeable and [he] can absorb pages of instructions at lightning speed', 'involved in a number of highly contentious matters', 'singled out for his work for large blue-chip companies', 'combination of in-depth legal knowledge, pragmatism, quick response times and approachability', 'inexhaustible', 'tenacious', 'knowledgeable', and 'an excellent advocate'.

He is one of the leading speakers and trainers on the employment law and HR circuit. He has presented seminars for the House of Commons, the BBC, Oxford University, HSBC, Barclays Bank, Ocado, and dozens of other organisations in-house. In 2013, 2014, 2016, and 2019 he designed — and was the sole speaker at — the Employment Law MasterClass national tour.

As well as full-time practice as a barrister and speaker, Daniel is the founder of the HR Inner Circle – a membership club for smart, ambitious HR Professionals. In 2007, he co-founded CPD Webinars Ltd, then the UK's leading webinar training company for lawyers, and sold it to Thomson Reuters in 2011.

Daniel is widely sought after as a commentator in both broadcast and print media on all legal issues. Since 2010 he has presented the Legal Hour on LBC Radio. In 2019, he launched Employment Law Matters, a weekly podcast with short explanations of employment law topics. Subscribe at www.danielbarnett.co.uk/podcast

www.danielbarnett.co.uk
Temple, London

Contents

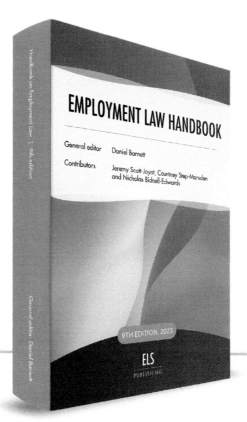

Introduction

Problem employees have been around for as long as the 'master and servant' relationship has existed. The vast majority of employees – and probably all HR practitioners – could tell a story about having worked with, managed or encountered one. Everyone's probably had a moment at work where, with reflection, they would have responded differently to a situation if they'd had their time again.

It's usually straightforward to categorise employee problems as capability or misconduct issues and address them accordingly. However, there's less clarity about behaviour that isn't obviously one or the other but is a problem nonetheless. Employers are wary of taking action that might result in a claim, and, as with so many 'minor' issues, the time spent dealing with a problem employee can be disproportionate to the seriousness of the issue itself. It can open up a can of worms and expose greater problems, with the result that sometimes employers prefer to ignore the problem and hope it goes away. Sometimes that's exactly what happens, with the voluntary departure of one or more of the parties involved.

The risk, though, is that the employer loses good employees and that the remaining staff are left dissatisfied that a situation wasn't dealt with. Where all the employees remain, the behaviour can be frustrating and can result in reduced morale, disputes at work or rash management decisions taken just to do something, all of which can result in costly employment tribunal claims.

The statistics for employment tribunal claims make interesting reading. In the quarter from July to September 2023, there were around 7,400 single employment tribunal claims received, and around 12,000 multiple claims received [Source:]. On average, a successful unfair dismissal claim resulted in an award of £11,914, with discrimination claims ranging from an average of £14,210 (age) to £45,435 (disability). For the vast majority of small and medium-sized businesses in the UK, those figures could be crippling.

Employment tribunal claims show little sign of slowing down. Employers must clearly outline the steps they take in order to successfully defend such claims.

This book deals with problem employees and their dismissal. Employers are often frustrated about how much problem behaviour they have to put up with before they can dismiss. It's important to say at the outset that dismissal can be an option in these circumstances. As with every dismissal, preparation and documentation is key to making sure no claim arises.

What is a 'problem employee'?

Consider first what a problem employee is. For the purposes of this book, a problem employee is defined as an employee who demonstrates behaviour that isn't necessarily misconduct or poor performance and that is perhaps not sufficiently serious to warrant formal disciplinary or performance management action, but which is nonetheless annoying or disruptive in some way.

Many behaviours can fall within this definition, from anti-social or work-shy behaviour to personality clashes or the repeated submission of complaints or grievances. At the more serious end of the scale, there is the expression of views that perhaps don't fit with others' views or the organisation's values: different political opinions, opinions on current affairs and the expression of gender-critical views.

You may find it difficult to start conversations with staff who engage in problem behaviour. Who wants to give the news that someone is a problem in the workplace? As with any HR-related situation, making a workable plan is half the battle. Planning allows you to reflect on:

- What the problem really is

- Any environmental factors that are triggering or exacerbating it

- Whether it is a new issue or something that the organisation has allowed to fester

- Whether there are any personal issues at play (and if so, what to do about them)

- Whether there are training needs or reasonable adjustments that could be made

In the end, good planning allows you to decide whether the problem is unlikely to go away unless more decisive action is taken.

It's also essential to have documented evidence to hand if an employment tribunal claim does arise. A contemporaneous record of your consideration and investigation will show your willingness to work through the problem, which is something employment tribunals will expect to see. All of these things combat suggestions of unfairness in decision-making or pre-determined decisions.

It's always a bold step to dismiss a problem employee, and it's usually a last resort, but it's possible and sometimes necessary in the best interests of the business.

This book examines various 'problem employee' situations, considers suitable approaches to address them, and looks at the risks that can arise. It also considers risk management and dealing with an employment tribunal claim if one arises.

1. The law relating to problem employees

There's nothing different or new about the law as it relates to problem employees or their dismissal. Matters are still dealt with in the same way and under the same legislation.

Time limits

The same time limits apply to dismissals or other claims in problem employee matters as apply elsewhere. Early conciliation must commence by the date that is three months less one day from the date that employment ends, or from the date of the last discriminatory act if that is earlier.

Early conciliation with Acas lasts for a maximum of six weeks. There is then an extension of time based on the length of early conciliation.

An employment tribunal may extend the time limit if it is missed, but only where there is good reason to do so. The grounds and arguments are more complex than that, of course, but this gives a general overview of the way that time limits apply. See book 4 in this series, 'Time Limits in Employment Tribunal Litigation', for more information (available via www.danielbarnett.com – look under 'Books' > 'Employment Law Library' – or via Amazon).

Early conciliation

An aggrieved employee who has been dismissed or feels they've been subject to discrimination will still be expected to go through Acas early conciliation before issuing any claim. Keep in mind that there are limited exceptions to that requirement, but in general, it's the first requirement. There is an option to bypass the conciliation element and simply request the certificate, so the first you may know of an employee's issues about their treatment and/or dismissal may be receipt of a claim.

Employers can start early conciliation too, although fewer than 5% of notifications started this way between July and September 2023 [Source: Early conciliation and employment tribunal data for England, Scotland, and Wales: July to September 2023 (Acas)]. Employers in this situation may wish to start early conciliation because settling a potential claim before it even gets off the ground can be a huge reassurance. It's a different approach to offering a settlement agreement, but there are circumstances where it can work just as well (or better) than involving a lawyer, particularly if all parties just want a quick resolution and there is no need to include complex terms, such as restrictive covenants, in any settlement agreement.

A recent example of this comes from an HR Inner Circle member. They advised an employer to start early conciliation because the employee showed no sign of returning to work following a disagreement and the nature of their complaint (raised as a grievance) was such that it was clear the employment relationship had irretrievably broken down and a tribunal claim was likely. While it was early to involve Acas, the conciliation process ultimately resulted in a successful resolution for all parties, avoiding lengthy internal processes and litigation. There's a good chance that matters will end there. Acas reports that around 72% of early conciliation notifications do not result in the submission of a claim, so the odds seem to be in the employer's favour, either because they reach a settlement or because the employee chooses not to pursue the matter.

Employment Rights Act 1996

The *Employment Rights Act 1996* (ERA) sets out the basis for dismissing an employee fairly. An employer must follow a fair procedure and reach its decision based on a fair and reasonable consideration of the evidence. Potential reasons for which an employer can fairly dismiss are conduct, capability, illegality, redundancy and some other substantial reason (SOSR). SOSR can be a useful option in these situations, and it is explored more closely later in the chapter.

If you get to the point of dismissal and then receive a claim, an employment tribunal will expect to see compliance with the ERA, and will look for:

- A reasonable investigation

- (In most cases) an opportunity to improve

- (Usually) written invitations to disciplinary hearings, with appropriate warnings about the most severe sanctions that might be applied

- The right of appeal

- Where there is a dismissal, a fair reason for that dismissal

Where the dismissal is for alleged problem behaviour, a tribunal will also look for genuine consideration of how dismissal could be avoided through steps such as redeployment, changes in working arrangements or mediation (*Turner v. Vestric Ltd [1980] ICR 528* and *Miller v. University of Bristol ET/1400780/2022 5 February 2024*).

The Equality Act 2010

The *Equality Act 2010* is the other main act to keep in mind. Some behaviours might be a manifestation of protected characteristics and any action or dismissal connected to those characteristics could result in a discrimination claim. This could arise from the more commonly encountered characteristics such as disability or pregnancy, or, as is prevalent in the media at the moment, the expression of political or philosophical beliefs, and how employers balance the right to express beliefs with the risk of other employees being offended by those beliefs.

The Acas Code of Practice

The *Acas Code of Practice on Disciplinary and Grievance Procedures* (the Acas Code) applies to 'disciplinary situations'. Such situations include formal disciplinary hearings and might also include SOSR dismissals. Unsurprisingly, it's safer to assume that it does apply, and that is where the bulk of the case law points at present.

Procedural fairness is always advisable, though, not to mention good employment relations practice. Employers should follow the principles of the Acas Code even if it means doing more than the law requires.

There's nothing new in any of the applicable law, the Acas Code or the expectations upon employers. What is potentially trickier is showing that the decision to dismiss was reasonable to take.

Key cases

The case law doesn't change, so by way of a very quick reminder, here are the key cases to keep in mind:

1. *British Home Stores Limited v. Burchell [1978] IRLR 379*

2. *Iceland Frozen Foods Limited v. Jones [1982] IRLR 439*

These two cases set out the tests that are applied in claims of unfair dismissal. A dismissal for misconduct will only be fair if, at the time of dismissal:

- The employer believed the employee to be guilty of misconduct.

- The employer had reasonable grounds for believing that the employee was guilty of that misconduct.

- At the time it held that belief, the employer had carried out as much investigation as was reasonable.

The tribunal must then decide whether the employer's decision to dismiss fell within the 'band of reasonable responses'.

Where the reason for the dismissal is alleged to be poor performance or capability, in the language of the ERA, the employer must show:

- A reasonable belief that the employee isn't capable of doing their job

- That its managers didn't fail in discharging their own responsibilities to the employee, which means showing that the employer's expectations about the role and how to perform it were provided, together with any necessary support or training.

Polkey v. AE Dayton Services Ltd [1987] IRLR 503 allows an employer to argue that a compensatory award in the event of a successful unfair dismissal claim should be reduced, where the claimant would have been dismissed in any event and therefore any procedural errors by the employer would have made no difference. A *Polkey* reduction in compensation doesn't make a dismissal fair, but if the tribunal accepts an argument for a reduction, it will take into account what might have happened in the future and award compensation accordingly. It's not a licence for poor employer conduct, which any tribunal will still scrutinise closely when considering an unfair dismissal claim, but it's helpful to know about it and be able to raise it in response to a claim.

There is a great deal of other case law, of course, but these are the headline points. Being aware of the applicable law and the key case law will stand employers and HR practitioners in good stead to argue that a dismissal was fair.

2. What's the problem … and is there a problem with the problem?

Unfortunately, problem employees don't come with a label attached or any other identifying features, so when complaints are first raised about an employee, it's a good idea to ask yourself a few preliminary questions:

- **What** is the problem behaviour?

- **Who** is causing the problem and whose problem is it?

- **Where** is the problem behaviour coming from?

- **Why** is the problem behaviour arising?

- **What** can be done about it?

What type of problems can constitute problem behaviour?

For the purposes of this book, a 'problem employee' is someone who displays behaviour that becomes annoying, irritating or distracting over time rather than someone who overtly displays behaviour that could amount to capability or conduct reasons for disciplinary action and dismissal. Unaddressed issues can fester and grow, so it's important for employers to feel confident in addressing issues before that happens.

Examples can cross a wide scale and can include:

- Negative behaviour
- Argumentative or challenging behaviour
- Personality clashes
- Being over-talkative, or not talkative at all
- Being easily distracted from work or is slow at completing their tasks
- Repeatedly raising grievances or informal complaints
- Having the 'wrong' attitude
- Expressing views that some people might find offensive, for example, in relation to politics, race or life choices

What it means to be 'over talkative' to one person might be just right to someone else. This makes it more complex and more important than ever to investigate and base the decision on facts and not subjective feelings or personality.

Problem behaviour doesn't always only occur in the workplace either. It might happen at work-related events, or on social media in the form of 'liked' comments or pictures, re-circulated posts or original posts that others might find offensive. If there's a close enough connection with the workplace, the employer can still address it.

Is it my problem?

A harsh question to ask, perhaps, but one to consider at an early stage. Most day-to-day grumbles are for line managers to deal with. A line manager's clear and prompt intervention could be all that is required. Escalating the problem to another party, such as HR, is often unnecessary and counterproductive.

Before beginning any type of investigation, consider whether you are the right person to deal with the matter, particularly if you're somehow involved in the context. Of course, if you're the sole HR Manager in a small business, there might be no way around it, but if there is an alternative, it's worth considering whether someone else should address the problem.

Acas offers a helpful guidance note on 'Conducting Challenging Conversations', which offers practical guidance on how to prepare yourself.

Understand what the problem actually is – is there a problem with the problem?

An informal investigation

It is fundamentally important to understand the **actual** problem. The immediately apparent problem may not be the real issue at all, but only a thorough consideration of events and facts can reveal that.

With that in mind, as usual, your starting point is an investigation. There is a curious contrast here, though. On one hand, the investigation is unlikely to be a formal investigation, at least at this stage – you just won't know if it might result in formal action against anyone. On the other hand, it's an investigation that needs to be quite forensic to enable you to understand the context of the problem behaviour. It's only when you understand the context that you can identify the next steps.

It can often be helpful to think about your organisation's expected values. Does the behaviour misalign with them? This can often give those dealing with such matters a strong foundation to start the difficult conversation.

Carrying out a thorough investigation ensures that you speak to all involved parties, not just the alleged problem employee, and looking for the context of the behaviour may reveal facts that weren't previously apparent. Think about, for example, the existence of a clique that might have isolated the alleged problem employee, resulting in that employee becoming withdrawn or surly. A victim of bullying may change their behaviour, perhaps becoming more negative about things or quieter and slower in their work.

What may appear to be a problem at first glance may, of course, be a manifestation of a protected characteristic. Consider, for example, an employee with neurodiversity, where one or more of the features of that neurodiversity is behaviour that is different from that of colleagues without that disability. Employees may perceive cultural differences as problem behaviour if they are unfamiliar or unaccustomed to each other's ways of life. For example, resentment around an employee taking time to pray or resentment at restrictions around permitted prayer times are both potential issues that can arise from cultural differences but which may not be immediately apparent.

Think too about personality clashes. Some people just don't get on. They wouldn't be friends outside of work and they find it difficult to work together. You can't force them to be friends, but an informal investigation could perhaps elicit information from one or both of them about why they find the other person to be a problem.

This is a problem – do something!

When a problem becomes too significant to ignore, it's time to act. At this stage, doing nothing is often the worst possible option.

But what **can** you do?

Assuming you've started your investigation as set out above, the path forward should hopefully become a little clearer. It may even be clear enough to enable you to categorise the behaviour as conduct or poor performance.

Here's an example. A neurodiverse employee suddenly stopped speaking to a colleague after the colleague pointed out a minor error the employee made. No harm was done, but nonetheless, the incident was correctly reported to a line manager for safety records. The employee said their colleague was wrong to report the incident because they're open about their neurodiversity and had previously agreed that discussions about them would take place with them, which they took to mean with **only** them. In the employee's view, the colleague telling their line manager was a breach of that agreement.

The employee's resulting behaviour towards their colleague is annoying, perhaps even upsetting, but should you treat it as a disciplinary matter? The answer is probably no, particularly considering the employee's protected characteristic, but you need to do **something** because doing nothing could suggest it's okay for an employee to stop speaking to a colleague and place you at risk of grievances from the colleague, and perhaps from the aggrieved employee too.

A general investigation could bring all this to light and prompt a review of the adjustments made for that employee and training provision for all concerned. More importantly, it could help you avoid inadvertently categorising disability-related behaviour as a 'problem' with related disciplinary or dismissal action. Taking the time to understand the problem behind the problem is an essential step in risk management.

When different, and sometimes problematic, behaviour is a result of a disability, employers are often understandably reluctant to take any action because of the disability. It can result in the behaviour continuing to go unchallenged, with the employee perhaps unaware that there are concerns. That was the case in *Lydall v. The Wooldridge Partnership ET/3314738/2021*, where it was not made clear to the claimant that her performance was considered sub-standard before her dismissal and where an award of over £32,000 in compensation was made. It's an employment tribunal case only, so isn't binding on other tribunals, but it's a good example of how a failure to properly consider the cause of poor performance can come back to haunt an employer.

Here's another example involving a long-standing employee of a company. The employee knows their job and does it well. What they don't do so well is adapt to change, and this has become more apparent with the introduction of new systems and a new, younger, line manager. The employee attends training but sits at the back and makes it obvious they're there under sufferance, before returning to work and doing exactly as they have before.

Again, this is annoying and frustrating behaviour, but is it sufficient to discipline or start performance management proceedings? That's debatable because it may amount to a deliberate refusal to follow a reasonable management request, which is a conduct matter, but what's the **something** you can do to break the deadlock before taking disciplinary action? Again, it's best to start with an informal investigation of the issue to better understand the employee's reluctance to adapt. It could be fear of redundancy or of not understanding new systems and technologies, or the employee could even be the subject of age-inappropriate comments from other colleagues about their ability to cope with new demands. Such an investigation allows you an opportunity to make clear that non-compliance isn't an option and hint that disciplinary action could be on the horizon.

Of course, not all problem behaviour has a context. Sometimes, an employer will come across an employee who, for no real reason, just isn't right for the job. The employer may not be able to put their finger on why, and sometimes, it'll be because there's no issue but the employee just doesn't want to be there and is determined to let everyone know it.

Whilst any investigation should be compassionate and thorough, guard against any temptation to anticipate the reasons behind the behaviour or make excuses for poor behaviour. If there is a cause, the employee should have the opportunity to tell you, but their behaviour should not be at the expense of the wider good of the company. You should always set conversations against the background of 'there's something here that we need to fix'.

Hope v. British Medical Association (EAT/2021/187) raises some interesting points in relation to dismissal for alleged problem behaviour. The BMA dismissed Mr Hope on grounds of gross misconduct after raising multiple grievances over the course of several months, and on the basis that his misuse of the grievance procedure had become a matter of misconduct.

The case is due to be heard by the Court of Appeal later this year (2024), and it's hoped that it will provide guidance on whether problem behaviour can ever be regarded as gross misconduct, to enable dismissal without warning, as happened to Mr Hope. Should the BMA have formally warned Mr Hope that his conduct was becoming unacceptable? Mr Hope raised these concerns over several months, and – arguably – the opportunity was there to give those warnings, although it's questionable whether Mr Hope would have heeded them. Hopefully, the Court of Appeal will also comment on the view of the Employment Appeal Tribunal (EAT) that grievance procedures are not a "repository for complaints that can then be left unresolved and capable of being resurrected at any time at the behest of the employee".

Does this create a situation where an employer can effectively say to a permanently (or repeatedly) aggrieved employee "Put up or shut up" and regard a grievance as withdrawn if it is not formally pursued? There's also the question of whether, in fact, Mr Hope's grievances were legitimate. The tribunal found that the employer had carried out a fair investigation that satisfied the standard tests in *BHS v. Burchell* and *Iceland Frozen Foods*, but that was in relation to the disciplinary action. There was clearly frustration about Mr Hope's conduct, but was the **reason** for his conduct lost or overlooked? And would a different investigative approach to his grievances have produced a different outcome? There may never be an answer to that, but a wise employer should certainly keep in mind the reason why everything began in the first place and make sure they've dealt with that thoroughly.

After you've identified the problem behaviour and started an investigation, the next step is to consider how to address the behaviour and prevent recurrence. To learn more about investigations, please see book 1 in this series, 'Employee Investigations' for more information (available via www.danielbarnett.com – look under 'Books' > 'Employment Law Library' – or via Amazon).

There are benefits of having alternatives to formal 'sanctions' and dismissal built into performance management and disciplinary policies. These range from mediation and team building to informal performance improvement plans linked to behaviour. None of these are new, but they can be highly effective.

3. How should you address problem behaviour and prevent recurrence?

As stated in Chapter 2, there's nothing different about the law that applies to so-called problem employees. If they are dismissed – and assuming they have the requisite two years' service – they can bring an unfair dismissal claim. Even if they don't have two years' service, they may be able to bring a discrimination claim, if they allege protected characteristics to be the 'real' reason for the dismissal. An aggrieved employee could also explore whether one of the other categories of automatic unfair dismissal applies. It can be easy to overlook those in circumstances where the employee has less than two years' service and all seems straightforward, but it's important to remember that whistleblowing and discrimination can also be used as grounds for an unfair dismissal claim.

Investigate

The investigation process will almost certainly start with an informal chat with those involved to try to get to the bottom of what's happening and what's causing the problem behaviour.

Sometimes, the problem and its cause are obvious, requiring only an informal investigation. However, on some occasions, there will be a need for a deeper dive. Any investigation needs to meet the usual standards expected and envisaged by *BHS v. Burchell* and *Iceland Frozen Foods*. In this vague category of not-quite-misconduct or not-quite-underperformance, it is sensible to pay particular attention to the content of your investigation to ensure you properly identify the problem and what the risks to your company might be.

Here's an example involving low-level dissatisfaction with a fairly new employee.

"They never join in" goes the complaint. "They're so isolated and miserable; they don't fit in."

On the face of it, the complaints are similar and could indicate someone who just doesn't want to be at work. But an investigation might reveal counter-issues, such as a clique of existing employees that is (unwittingly or otherwise) excluding the new employee, who, as a result, feels isolated and miserable. Or it might reveal a previously undisclosed disability, or language or cultural differences. All these things can be addressed through support and/or training, rendering a dismissal unnecessary.

Document everything

Documenting your findings is important in this type of situation as you may need to explain your reasoning to an employment tribunal. Referring to contemporaneous notes setting out your thought processes, decisions and reasons is often crucial to successfully defending a claim. Recording what others have said about the behaviour and its impact on them is also crucial to your decision-making processes. Remember that every document, WhatsApp message, text and email could potentially be evidence in an employment tribunal. Remember you can't prove what was said during a phone call unless you note it down at the time.

The risks of an unfair investigation

A dismissal can be rendered unfair if the employment tribunal decides the investigation process is flawed in some way, so documenting what you have done and why can help to avoid any suggestion of an unfair process. Keep in mind that an unfair investigation may even give an employee grounds to resign and claim constructive dismissal.

That was the claim in *Retirement Security Ltd v. Miss A Wilson [UKEAT] 0019/19*, in which Miss Wilson was suspended immediately after complaints by three managers who reported to her. She then had less than 24 hours' notice of an investigation meeting because the invitation letter was sent to the wrong address. Further procedural errors meant she was initially told her line manager would support her but later learned they would be chairing the meeting. Finally, she received no documents prior to the investigation meeting. Miss Wilson resigned, stating that the company clearly no longer had any trust in her and that she had not been given a fair chance to respond to the allegations. Her claim for constructive dismissal succeeded and the EAT upheld it when the employer appealed.

Avoid knee-jerk reactions

It's especially important to avoid 'knee-jerk' reactions. It may be abundantly clear that frustrated employees want the behaviour to stop but rushing into a reaction can sometimes be counter-productive.

It's important to consider whether the alleged problem employee has strengths that can be used. Are they valuable to your business and is there an opportunity to make use of their skills? Playing to the strengths of all employees can sometimes offer a solution. Take the example of the employee constantly offering unsolicited advice – which is in the worked examples below. Can you move them to a part of the business where their suggestions can be tested, or would at least be welcomed?

Informal action

If the problem behaviour is low-level or you've addressed it at an early stage, it's worth considering informal resolution too. Is there training, support or coaching you can offer to highlight the employee's strengths and provide them with mechanisms to modify the behaviours that are causing concern?

Consider whether mediation might be an option, either as an internal exercise or with a mediator. Mediation can take many forms and can be especially useful for personality clashes, offering the opportunity for individual discussions with each employee to attempt to reach a solution.

With such practical suggestions, it's important to carefully consider whether they will work and use them in the hope that they will. Such practical approaches can show an employment tribunal that you explored all possible options and solutions before deciding to dismiss and that there was nothing else you could reasonably do.

Formal action

Not every investigation will produce a clear reason for the problem behaviour, nor will every proposed solution result in a workforce that is once again happy and content. As and when you face that situation, the only option is to take formal action.

Procedurally, nothing is different from any other formal action you might take. To a certain extent, you will need to nail your colours to the mast of conduct or poor performance at this stage, as the letter of invitation to the hearing will need to set out what the behaviour is and what rules it contravenes. A tribunal will expect to see a written invitation to a hearing, whether disciplinary or capability, setting out the behaviour in question and providing examples so the employee knows what allegations they are facing. Normally, failure to follow this essential part of the process places employers at risk of a finding of procedurally unfair dismissal, although there are cases where employers have successfully contested unfair dismissal claims despite not having followed any procedure.

In *Gallacher v. Abelio Scotrail Ltd UKETS/0027/19*, the EAT upheld a dismissal on grounds of SOSR despite no procedure having been followed as a result of a complete breakdown in working relations between Mrs Gallacher and her line manager, and where she was told during her appraisal that she was being 'exited'. The EAT considered that this was a case where following proper procedures would be futile because a good working relationship was so essential to the respondent business.

Similarly, in *Moore v. Phoenix Product Development Ltd EAT/0070/20*, another SOSR dismissal was upheld despite the employee not being offered any right of appeal. The EAT considered that as the employee was a board-level director and the company was small, with no higher level of management, the absence of an appeal did not make her dismissal unfair, particularly in circumstances where the employee was described as 'unrepentant'.

These are unusual examples and not recommended practice, but they're worth knowing about in case you discover procedural irregularities following a dismissal carried out without HR intervention. It's much safer to follow the normal process and make sure everything is properly documented.

To warn or not to warn?

Unless your employee is manifesting behaviour that amounts to gross misconduct, or unless they have less than two years' service and you're comfortable that their problematic behaviour isn't the result of protected characteristics or whistleblowing, then usually you will need to consider issuing warnings.

In most cases, an employment tribunal will expect to see evidence that you have informed the employee about their behaviour and the problems it causes, together with a requirement that they modify their behaviour. Consider carefully whether to offer support, training or recommendations for mediation. If you conclude that there is no support, training or mediation that will assist, then again, you should carefully document this in case you need to explain your decision-making in the future.

Dismissal

Dismissal isn't inevitable in situations of problematic behaviour, but it's something that does happen regularly, as the case law shows.

If you've exhausted warnings, or if you've decided that you need to conclude the matter quickly, the letter inviting the employee to a hearing should inform them that dismissal is a potential outcome. Paragraph 9 of the Acas Code requires that an employee is given sufficient information before a hearing to enable them to understand the allegations against them. *Boyd v. Renfrewshire Council [2008] CSIH 36* also confirmed that failure to notify an employee that they are effectively fighting for their job could render any subsequent dismissal unfair.

Where an employee has less than two years' service and you're comfortable (because of your investigation) that there are no protected characteristics to keep in mind, then a dismissal should be reasonably straightforward, with only a need to consider whether to pay notice pay or whether you intend to treat the behaviour as gross misconduct and summarily dismiss. Pay particular attention to your policies at this point and what you will provide as examples of misconduct and gross misconduct. Being able to link a summary dismissal to an example in the handbook might help you avoid a wrongful dismissal claim for notice pay.

Where the employee has two years' service or more, and/or where protected characteristics may be a factor, you must carefully consider and document the decision to dismiss, as well as the alternatives, such as redeployment and mediation. In *Miller*, a very recent case that involved dismissal for the expression of anti-

Zionist beliefs, the Bristol Employment Tribunal found the dismissal to be unfair for a number of reasons, including the employer's failure to adequately consider a sanction short of dismissal. That's why it's important to document all your points. Even if you don't think a lesser sanction would work, note that you've considered it and the reasons why you've discounted it in case you need it at the tribunal.

Reflection

Once the dust has settled after a dismissal, however it is resolved, it is always worth an internal debrief to identify how the situation arose and how to make sure it doesn't happen again.

Recruitment is, of course, a key part of that debrief. It's sensible to look at the processes applied and the assessment of an individual's 'fit' for the workplace. Evaluate onboarding and induction processes to make sure standards of conduct are made clear from the outset.

It's also a good time to review your policies and procedures:

- Do you have written discipline and grievance procedures? (If not, visit www.policies2024.com or find later iterations via www.danielbarnett.com.)

- Do they set out the standards of behaviour expected from staff?

- Do they clearly indicate that misuse of grievance procedures may be treated as a disciplinary matter?

Also, consider whether you use probationary periods and appraisals appropriately and sensibly. It is often possible to dismiss during a probationary period because there will usually be less than two years' service, although it's important to be as sure as possible that the perceived problem behaviour is not caused by protected characteristics.

Addressing problem behaviour in appraisals is more of a challenge. Holding difficult or challenging conversations is never easy, but it's often easier than having to conduct an avoidable dismissal conversation. The key to holding a challenging conversation during an appraisal is preparation. A manager should allow time and space for the conversation and have examples to hand of the behaviour in question. It is helpful to think about ways in which the behaviour can improve.

4. Risk management

What if you can't resolve the problem?

It's time to explore the crucial question: what if you can't resolve the problem? Is it ever possible to dismiss an employee for 'problem behaviour'? The answer, of course, is yes, and it may be essential to the business that you do. The important thing is risk management. As HR practitioners often point out, speed and risk are disproportionate to each other in an employment law context – the quicker the company wants something done, the greater the risk it may have to take.

There are a number of options open to employers when they have reached the point of no return. Dismissal is only one of those options and is obviously the riskiest because it can bring with it the potential of an employment tribunal claim.

Employer-led early conciliation

Acas early conciliation is always available, and employer-led early conciliation has also been available since its inception in April 2014 but is much less commonly used.

This might be an appealing option for an employer, over a settlement agreement because it can be quick, straightforward and informal – and there may be no need to involve lawyers, which is often a winner. See more about Acas early conciliation in Chapter 1.

Settlement agreement

A settlement agreement is a tried and tested way of ensuring that there is no employment tribunal claim against the employer, and the terms and timetable are entirely a matter for the employer and employee to agree, so other factors can be included within the agreement.

Either party can introduce the possibility of a settlement agreement into discussions, either as a standalone option or as an alternative to dismissal – making sure, of course, to avoid any suggestion of 'improper behaviour' by placing improper pressure on an employee to accept the agreement.

As with the applicable legislation, there is nothing different about holding a protected conversation in the context of problem behaviour, nor offering a settlement agreement. Remember to ensure that there is a break between the substantive conversation about the allegations and the offer of the settlement agreement and to introduce the protected conversation as such. Acas offers helpful guidance and template documents to assist.

Dismissal

By the time you get to a possible dismissal, and particularly where an employee has more than two years' service, you should have followed the usual steps prior to a dismissal, which are:

- You have (usually) issued warnings previously and assisted in improving the behaviour.

- You have invited the employee to a hearing at which they have the right to be accompanied by a work colleague or a trade union representative.

- You have listened to any representations made by the employee about their behaviour.

- You have offered the right of appeal.

Dismissal with notice

If an employee has less than two years' service and you're comfortable that there are no protected characteristics and no suggestion of whistleblowing or health and safety-related dismissals, then another option is to either reach agreement with the employee that they will leave or dismiss them with notice.

It's unlikely (but not impossible) that problem behaviour of this nature would amount to gross misconduct, and of course, an employee who is summarily dismissed may be more aggrieved and therefore more likely to try to find ways to bring a claim if only to secure their notice pay, so a dismissal with notice can be a more palatable course of action. Even if you decide to dismiss with notice (and it is recommended that you do), there is no guarantee the employee won't still take advice about any potential claims or do their own research and conclude there is a claim to pursue, with the effect that you still need to deal with a claim.

Dismissal without notice

There may be circumstances where the behaviour is such a problem that you feel it is appropriate to treat it as gross misconduct or gross negligence. These would probably be unusual circumstances, and the behaviour would need to be pretty intolerable for it to amount to gross misconduct or negligence, but it may include things such as a refusal to modify the manner in which potentially controversial beliefs are expressed, although not usually the holding of those beliefs. If the behaviour damages relationships, then it may be possible to argue that any lesser sanction would be futile and a gross misconduct dismissal is the only solution.

Again, where there are two years' service or protected characteristics, you'll need to follow the usual procedural steps of having a hearing and considering your decision carefully. Make time to look at your policies and make sure there is a basis for your decision.

You've got a claim – now what?

Sometimes, despite the best planning and the most sympathetic of investigations and processes, employers can still receive a claim. Short of agreeing to a settlement when you don't want to, there's nothing you can do to prevent this. When an employee feels aggrieved, they want to be heard, and that's when effective planning and documentation become essential.

Capability or misconduct?

As mentioned, there are only five potentially fair reasons for dismissal. Capability and conduct are two of those, and the employer must establish which one they want to rely on as the reason for the employee's dismissal.

To a certain extent, by the point of dismissal, or at least by the point of responding to the claim, an employer will need to identify the behaviour they consider they've been dealing with. SOSR is sometimes used as an alternative reason.

In some cases, the label for the dismissal may not be entirely clear, and whilst it's important to be clear in the allegations made so the employee has the opportunity to respond to them, it is also open to a tribunal to find that a dismissal was fair, but for a different reason than the one pleaded by the employer. See, for example,

Screene v. Seatwave Ltd UKEAT/0020/11, where the EAT agreed that the tribunal was able to find a dismissal for those different reasons.

Some other substantial reason (SOSR)

SOSR can be the HR practitioner's friend in this situation. Why? Because it may not be obvious whether the behaviour is misconduct or capability, or a bit of both. Sometimes, the facts will point in the direction of one or the other, but not always, and where there is an element of doubt, SOSR can come to the rescue as the reason for dismissal.

SOSR is found at section 98(1)(b) of the ERA, and is defined as:

> *"some other substantial reason of a kind such as to justify the dismissal of an employee holding the position which the employee held."*

SOSR is often described as the 'catch-all' reason for dismissal when no other potentially fair reasons seem to apply. There's no statutory definition or guidance on what might amount to an SOSR dismissal, so employers, HR practitioners and their lawyers must look to the case law to try to work out where to use it. In the context of problem behaviour, it's useful to know that SOSR exists and the parameters within which you can use it.

An employment tribunal considering an SOSR defence to a claim must apply a two-stage test:

i. The employer has the burden of proof of showing that SOSR was the sole or principal reason for dismissal. Bear in mind that at this stage, all the employer must do is establish a reason that could justify the dismissal, not that it did justify it. At this stage, the tribunal can't consider any justification or potential fairness of the dismissal. To do so would be to conflate the two-stage test into one and risk making their decision appealable.

ii. The employer must show that the decision to dismiss for SOSR was reasonable in all the circumstances, including the size and resources of their undertaking. The burden of proof is neutral at this second stage, so the employer doesn't have to establish that it was reasonable and the employee doesn't have to establish that it was not. Instead, the tribunal will determine the question in accordance with equity (fairness) and the merits of the case, in line with section 98(4) of the ERA.

So, how does an employer establish SOSR? An employment tribunal certainly won't accept it lightly: the inclusion of the word 'substantial' is an indicator of that. Depending on the context of the problem behaviour, an employer will need to show behaviour that is causing serious or significant disruption to a business. An employer will also need to show that it has taken reasonable steps to resolve the problem, such as redeployment, altering work patterns to keep conflicted employees apart or attempting negotiation steps, such as mediation (see *Treganowan v. Robert Knee and Co Ltd, [1975] ICR 405 QBD* and *Turner*). Without those attempts, an employer may fail to establish that a dismissal was fair.

Responding to a claim – misconduct, poor performance, SOSR or a combination?

Employers should always consider whether there is any overlap between SOSR and one of the other potentially fair reasons for dismissal. By the time of a potential dismissal, it may be clearer that the problem behaviour could also be a matter of misconduct or poor performance. Raising SOSR and either misconduct or poor performance in your response to a claim allows you to argue that either could apply.

It is something that employers sometimes do. In *Ezsias v. North Glamorgan NHS Trust UKEAT/0399/09*, the employer argued that the employee's dismissal was because relationships had broken down (i.e. the dismissal was the **consequence** of the behaviour) and the tribunal accepted that as an SOSR dismissal. If the employer had focused on the employee's culpability for that breakdown (the behaviour being the **cause** of the breakdown and therefore the reason for the dismissal), SOSR may not have succeeded as the dismissal may instead have been for conduct reasons.

This was also the finding in *Perkin v. St George's Healthcare NHS Trust [2005] EWCA Civ 1174*, in which the Court of Appeal held that dismissing an employee because of his difficult personality could not of itself amount to SOSR, but the ways in which his personality manifested itself through his behaviour and interactions with others could be SOSR or misconduct. It's a fine distinction between the trait itself and the consequences of the trait, but it's an important one to keep in mind.

Does the Acas Code apply?

The EAT has given conflicting commentary on this point. The Code applies to 'disciplinary situations', namely misconduct and poor performance. Redundancy and the non-renewal of a fixed-term contract are specifically excluded from the Code (Paragraph 1), but there is no specific mention of SOSR.

The most recent case on this point is *Rentplus UK Limited v. Coulson [2022] EAT 81*, in which the EAT doubted previous case law that said the Code could never apply to SOSR dismissals, and stated that if the employer believes there is misconduct or poor performance, then the Code will apply, even if the employer labels the matter throughout as one of SOSR.

Obviously, assuming that the Code will apply is always going to be the safest course of action. An employment tribunal will never criticise employers for making sure a disciplinary process is fair and thorough, particularly where that disciplinary action results in a dismissal.

Dealing with a claim: the importance of contemporaneous documents

Once employment tribunal proceedings commence, they are rarely withdrawn unless there is a settlement during the proceedings. Assuming the employer doesn't wish to offer any settlement, you'll need to start taking steps to prepare for the final hearing.

Hopefully, you've made – and retained – notes throughout the matter before the dismissal took place. Contemporaneous notes setting out your reasons for taking certain action and the statements of employees you've spoken to will be essential evidence as you prepare to defend your decisions.

Dealing with a claim: mid-proceedings settlements

Remember that Acas remains available throughout an employment tribunal matter, and a settlement is sometimes the commercially sensible action to take. During your planning and preparation, it's good practice to return to the question of settlement as part of the process, if only to look at costs versus risks and make sure that points of principle are not becoming more expensive and time-consuming than they should.

More about SOSR

To learn more about SOSR, see book 18 of the Employment Law Library, 'Some Other Substantial Reason' (available viawww.danielbarnett.com – look under 'Books' > 'Employment Law Library' – or via Amazon). It explores the various contexts in which SOSR can be used, such as business reorganisations, personality clash dismissals and more. It gives you the knowledge you need to avoid common legal pitfalls associated with SOSR dismissals. It also provides practical, step-by-step guidance for implementing fair SOSR procedures across different HR scenarios.

5. Worked examples

This chapter covers common examples of problem behaviour and how to deal with them.

The negative employee who has nothing positive to say

Nothing goes right for this employee. Whatever is happening to anyone else, they've had it worse, both personally and professionally. There is a regular litany of their woes, which over time, becomes distracting, lowers morale for others and can become annoying. Conversations are only ever one way, and this employee seems to have no interest in properly engaging with their colleagues and having a two-way conversation.

Whilst this behaviour doesn't appear to be either misconduct or poor performance, it is the type of behaviour that over time can wear other employees down. It's draining to encounter on a regular basis and can result in reduced morale around the workplace.

The starting point is to identify who is the problem. On the face of things, it would seem to be the miserable employee. They would certainly be your starting point for an investigation, and an informal approach is sensible at the start. Make sure you consider the second element of the 'who' question – whose problem is it? That might be difficult to identify until you converse with the employee because there might not be an immediately identifiable reason for their misery (which could preclude someone from investigating it).

After that, consider where the behaviour is manifesting itself. Presumably, it's in the workplace (although remember the link to work-related events and social media usage), but is there anywhere specific? An informal meeting to ask if everything is ok because they seem rather down could eventually elicit that sort of information, or even better, you could ask the question in regular appraisals.

Thoroughly exploring the 'where' and the 'why' of this type of behaviour might highlight reasons for it, and showing that you made attempts to find those reasons will also stand you in good stead if there is ultimately a tribunal claim.

Of course, not every employee is by nature gregarious and bouncy, and no employers should expect that they are. Different personalities are essential to any community, and the workplace is no different. But that can also make dealing with this type of problem behaviour particularly difficult because you need to consider that employee's particular personality and balance that against the effect it has on their colleagues.

Following your investigation, you'll need to consider what you're going to do about this behaviour. That will depend on what your investigation has elicited. Specific triggers of the problem behaviour are likely to be easier to address, for example, through coaching or support to address concerns about the workplace. Trickier is miserable behaviour that has no basis, or at least none that you can identify despite your sensitive and thorough investigation. This is likely to be the point where you will need to carefully handle a difficult conversation. If the behaviour is at the point where colleagues are raising complaints about it, then 'something' needs to be done, and the employee needs to be told their behaviour is negatively impacting colleagues and needs to change. A discussion can include ways that the employee can express their views that won't impact their colleagues and establish whether they appreciate the impact their behaviour is having.

The situation can then develop in one of several ways. Ideally, you'll see an effort to improve, but there could be a complete refusal to change or accept there is anything wrong or even a resignation and an attempt to claim constructive dismissal. That's where your documents enable you to show your conduct on behalf of the company was acceptable and unlikely to destroy or damage the relationship of trust and confidence.

As the situation develops, it may become slightly more straightforward to categorise the behaviour. It's a 'can't do/won't do' situation: if there is a willingness to improve but a lack of ability to do it, it's likely a poor performance situation ('can't do'), whereas a refusal to change is more likely a conduct issue ('won't do').

Whilst all dismissals should be carefully documented, a dismissal for this type of negative behaviour will need particularly careful recording. Showing that you've alerted the employee to their behaviour, explored possible explanations for their behaviour and found none, and required an improvement and none has been forthcoming will all assist in contesting an unfair dismissal or discrimination claim.

All of that takes time unless you take a riskier approach and dismiss without going through a formal process. If you prefer dismissal, you might consider a protected conversation to explain to the employee that they don't seem happy despite efforts to understand why and offers of assistance, and that it's preferable to go separate ways. In many cases, the proposal of a settlement agreement comes as no surprise and is often welcomed by an unhappy employee. As with all these situations, a departure with no ensuing tribunal claim is always the best outcome for all concerned.

The serial complainer / sometime grievance raiser

This employee is more overt than their miserable colleague. They perceive many comments as slights, they know their right to raise a grievance and they're not afraid to use it. But they're equally unafraid of simply making their concerns known to whoever is around, whether they want to know or not. Over time, this can affect morale and can be counter-productive because colleagues may not take their complaints seriously.

Even so, it's important that you consider the substance of each grievance carefully. Even if the frequency of the grievances or complaints becomes frustrating, be prepared to read each one and take a view on it. The last thing you want is to ignore a grievance that turns out to be a genuine complaint about something serious, particularly one of the protected situations that might amount to whistleblowing, such as a risk to health and safety.

Once again, you will need to start with an investigation to identify who the problem employee is. This might be as part of either the grievance procedure itself or an informal investigation to try to get further information about what is happening.

Whether you commence a formal grievance investigation may depend on the number of grievances previously received and the action taken in relation to those grievances. If the employee's behaviour is a problem, it's reasonably safe to assume there have been unfounded grievances before. Ideally, the outcome of one or more of those grievances should have made clear to the employee that their continued misuse of the grievance procedure to pursue unfounded complaints will not be tolerated and may result in disciplinary action, as was the approach in *Hope*.

If the employee has received that information, you could categorise any repeated misuse of the grievance procedure as a conduct issue, as failure to comply with a reasonable management instruction. But be wary of falling into the trap of moving directly to disciplinary action without at least looking at the grievance first. Even if the employee hasn't received that previous 'heads up' or warning, it's sensible to check your grievance procedure, as it may make clear that misuse of the grievance procedure could result in disciplinary action.

If you move to disciplinary action and the employee offers no plausible explanation for their behaviour, your next decision is to consider a sanction. A summary dismissal for gross misconduct is a bold move, and not one that an employer should take lightly, particularly where the employee has more than two years' service. That didn't stop the employer in *Hope v British Medical Association* from dismissing for gross misconduct. Note that the Court of Appeal will consider the case later this year (2024), and it's hoped their judgment will provide clarity on dismissal of employees in this situation.

Mr Hope raised several grievances over several months, following accusations of being "unprofessional and dismissive" by a more senior colleague, Mr Jewtha, regarding an email about another colleague, Ms Dunn.

After many months and many grievances, Mr Hope said he did not wish to pursue the matters formally at that stage but wanted to retain his ability to do so. He was given a deadline to decide whether to raise a formal grievance or withdraw. This prompted another grievance regarding what Mr Hope described as the "arbitrary deadline", and a further grievance against Ms Dunn, who expressed bullying concerns.

Mr Hope wanted his line manager to deal with the issues informally, but that was not possible as the grievance involved more senior management. Mr Hope also declined proposed meetings with Ms Dunn and was informed that continuing to abuse the grievance procedure could result in disciplinary action. This prompted a further grievance, this time to the Chair of the BMA. Mr Hope was informed that if there could not be an informal resolution, the matter would proceed to a formal grievance hearing. This prompted another grievance, this time about the threat of disciplinary action. Mr Hope then refused to attend the formal grievance hearing, which (rather unusually) proceeded in his absence and concluded that Mr Hope's conduct was "frivolous and vexatious" and an abuse of process by repeatedly raising grievances without following them through. The hearing dismissed Mr Hope's grievances and commenced disciplinary action, conducted by external counsel. Mr Hope was dismissed for gross misconduct and brought an unfair dismissal claim.

The tribunal decided that the dismissal was fair. Mr Hope was dismissed because of his conduct, a fair reason for dismissal, and there had been a reasonable investigation and procedure. The dismissal was within the band of reasonable responses. Mr Hope appealed. The EAT dismissed his grounds of appeal, which were largely centred upon the characterisation of gross misconduct. The EAT observed that Mr Hope had repeatedly raised grievances that were not informally resolved, but which he had tried to keep alive without pursuing them. His fear that his grievances would be "closed off" if they went to the formal stage was insufficient: the purpose of the grievance procedure was to resolve those concerns, not to hold them in abeyance until he wished to resurrect them.

It was clearly permissible for the tribunal to find that the BMA had acted within the range of reasonable responses when it concluded that attempts to misuse that procedure were frivolous and vexatious. The Court of Appeal's view will hopefully shed light on whether an employer can treat repeated grievances as a disciplinary matter and how far that can be enforced.

The employee who knows best

Remember the Harry Enfield character whose catchphrase was 'You don't want to do it like that; you want to do it like this!'?

This employee is happy to offer unsolicited advice on anything, particularly on other employees' working practices. If only everyone would do as they say, the business would run better, be more profitable and generally much better than it is now. The problem is that their colleagues don't appreciate their input and their manager finds it annoying. That's the problem behaviour.

Your informal investigation should begin with a discussion with the employee about their comments. When planning that conversation, consider whether they are actually saying anything worth pursuing. This is important because bringing an element of positivity into the first conversation could be a useful way to address the situation without it escalating.

Even if there are valid suggestions, an employee of this nature must understand that imposing their views on colleagues isn't appropriate, particularly if they're not in a management position. You'll also need to plan to explain that however well-intentioned their comments are, they're not acceptable and that a change in behaviour is needed. But it might be necessary to say that the comments are unacceptable, explain why and tell the employee that they must stop.

This is another 'can't do, won't do' scenario. Do you have an employee who recognises the need to change but isn't sure how to go about it – a 'can't do' potential performance matter? Or one who disputes any need for them to change – a 'won't do' potential conduct matter?

One of *Hope*'s grievances was that he was excluded from meetings as a reaction to the grievance itself. There is little indication of whether it was considered that he should be at those meetings and whether that might have made any difference to his sense of injustice, but it's an important point to consider in general – could the employee actually have a point? If so, the resolution of their repeated input could be to agree parameters around offering that input: when, where, how and to whom they will do it.

The resistor of change

This is the type of employee who has a lengthy service behind them and works to the mantra of 'this is how we've always done it'. They meet any new processes, practices or procedures with resistance, complaints and subtle refusal to comply.

There's a lot going on with this one. Change can be intimidating, and in an employment context, it can bring fear of redundancy or failure. Introduce any significant changes to the working environment carefully, with thought and with regard to any applicable obligations. Assuming you've done all that and have explained the reason for the change, given any necessary reassurances regarding the absence of redundancies or gone through a suitable redundancy procedure and offered all appropriate training and support, you're in a position to challenge the employee.

Going through that investigative process with the employee could be of particular importance here because there may be protected characteristics influencing the behaviour. For example, an older employee may fear that they will struggle with the change or a disabled employee may be concerned about the adjustments needed. Demonstrating the conversations that you've had, and the explanations given, will assist in showing that the business needed your requirement for all employees to embrace the change and that you've considered any potential discriminatory impact.

The employee who expresses controversial views

What of the employee who has strong opinions and sees no difficulty in airing them? It's a question arising more frequently at present, resulting in case law that is fascinating for lawyers and alarming for employers.

An employee dismissed or disciplined because of their beliefs could have a discrimination claim, so an investigation of the problem needs to be carried out extremely carefully. Employers need to understand the distinction between holding and expressing those views and how the views are manifested to colleagues.

Your investigation should begin with the individual who is expressing the views to discuss how others perceive their expression of their belief. It may be that they simply don't realise the impact of their actions and an informal conversation is sufficient to stop or adjust their behaviour.

Conversely, their belief may be so robust that they feel entitled to express it however they choose. There should then be a discussion with those who have raised complaints to understand precisely what they are complaining about: the fact that the particular views are held or how they are manifested.

There are no easy solutions here. Conversations with staff may help, and mediation is a possible means of repairing relationships. Appropriately worded warnings may also persuade an employee to think more carefully about how they express their opinions.

No employer finds this scenario easy to deal with. There are several recent cases on this point, but the case law goes back as far as 1975 in *Tregnanowan*, where similar issues were considered. *Tregnanowan* looked at the dismissal of an employee who gave frank disclosures regarding her sex life, creating an atmosphere that was, in the words of the tribunal "so tense that it was unbearable". Her dismissal was found to be fair, and the EAT agreed, saying that the business was small and had no real alternative. Over 30 years later, in *Ladele v. London Borough of Islington [2009] EWCA Civ. 1357, [2010] IRLR 211*, the dismissal of an employee, following competing views about sexual orientation and religion, was found to be fair on grounds of SOSR.

Much more recently, in *Phoenix v. The Open University ET3322700/21*, the tribunal upheld claims of direct discrimination, harassment, victimisation and constructive dismissal following Professor Phoenix's expression of gender-critical views. That decision was issued on 24 January 2024 and a remedy hearing is awaited.

There were similar findings in *Rachel Meade v. Westminster City Council and Social Work England ET2201792/22 and 2211483/22*, in which Ms Meade was found to have been harassed for expressing her gender-critical views. A remedy hearing is also awaited in that case. Note that the tribunal criticised the investigation, pointing to the lack of rigour and the willingness to accept the complaint against her as it was presented.

Looking at the 'problem' – and any problems within that alleged problem – is one of the best starting points for any employer faced with complaints about alleged problem employees because risks identified at an early stage are easier to manage than those identified at the point of issuing and receiving a claim.

6. Conclusion

There's little doubt that problem employees will be around forever. But the management of those employees doesn't need to be an additional problem. Employers and HR practitioners can feel reasonably comfortable in taking steps to address problems as long as they dealt with them in a sympathetic and organised way.

There is no replacement for thorough documentation and recording of events, witness evidence and thought processes. They act as a contemporaneous record of what you're doing and why you're doing it, and that's crucial if you're facing a tribunal claim. Such processes also often clear the mind and show a clear path to resolution. Dismissal isn't inevitable, and it's possible to resolve situations if all parties are willing to work towards resolving them.

When dismissal does become inevitable, though, it's important to remember some key principles:

- **Investigate**: look at what the problem is, whether it's the 'real' problem or whether something else underlying is affecting behaviours.

- **Allocate**: make sure the correct person is in place to address the issue from the start.

- **Discuss**: speak to the problem employee and those impacted by the behaviour.

- **Avoid knee-jerk reactions**: think things over. If the behaviour merits an urgent response, then it's likely to be a conduct issue and may warrant suspension whilst you complete an investigation.

- **Assess alternative resolution methods**: consider moving staff, changing hours and mediation.

- **Follow usual dismissal procedures**: provide written invitations to meetings, notification of the likely sanction (especially where dismissal is contemplated), the right to be accompanied and the right of appeal.

- **Keep records**: document, document, document!

- **Avoid panic**: early conciliation notifications or tribunal claims are sometimes speculatively brought, and you usually have the option of resisting a claim or considering a commercial resolution.

- **Reflect**: consider a reflective exercise once the dust has settled to look at how to avoid the same situation in the future.

Also by
Daniel Barnett

Available on Amazon
or visit
go.danielbarnett.com/books

JOIN DANIEL EVERY SATURDAY EVENING AT
9PM WHEN HE PRESENTS THE ALL-NEW

LBC LEGAL HOUR

— OR CATCH UP VIA THE GLOBAL PLAYER,
AT bit.ly/lbclegalhour

SATURDAYS, 9PM

Dear HR Professional,

I take my hat off to you.

Having supported the HR community for so many years, I know It's a challenging job you do, sometimes under really difficult circumstances.

The tricky HR issues you have to handle must take up a tremendous amount of your time, your energy and your brain power. I bet it can be exhausting for you to work under that level of pressure.

Being An HR Professional In Today's Business Environment Is TOUGH!

Maintaining your high standards of professionalism must be a real struggle, especially when your efforts and expertise often go unappreciated.

I'll wager you have to make decisions on challenging HR situations you've sometimes never encountered before. Even if you're part of a team, it must sometimes feel like you're working in isolation.

With so much complexity and ambiguity, do you ever find you're not clear whether you're doing the right thing when there's so much to think about?

I expect it can be draining too. You've got to make tough decisions which may be unpopular.

The pressure's on you to ensure people are treated fairly while the business complies with its legal obligations.

It's a thankless task, especially if you've got grief coming at you from all sides.

Doubt can creep in too. Even though you're an extremely competent professional, you might even begin to question yourself... What if you've got it wrong?

You've got to cope with all that, whilst constantly having to convince any doubting stakeholders you're adding value to the business.

That pressure must take its toll on you.

You wouldn't be human if it didn't cause you tension, stress or even worse!

Being the caring professional you are, I bet you often take work home with you.

If You're Not Careful The Stress WILL Creep Up On You

And I don't just mean opening your laptop on your couch when everyone else is watching Eastenders.

We all know of families and relationships that come a poor second to the pressures and challenges faced at work.

Yours too..?

But does it have to be that way?

Should you feel the responsibility of the HR world is entirely on your shoulders and that you've got to bear that burden alone?

The answer is a firm no.

It doesn't have to be like that.

There Is An Answer To Help Make Your Work & Your Life Much Easier For You

There's a place you can get all the help, support, advice and encouragement you need to ease the constant pressure you have to bear.

> It's called the
> HR Inner Circle.

It will lift the burden you're carrying by giving you swift access to comprehensive resources and live practical guidance you can implement right away.

It's information I know will save you time, energy and effort.

It's a vibrant, active community of caring, like minded HR professionals willing to help you.

There are resources packed full of practical, actionable advice for you that's difficult to find anywhere else.

And it doesn't matter what you're working on.

Whether it be workforce engagement, attracting and keeping talent, diversity and inclusion or employee health and well being, you'll find support for all of that.

You're covered even if you're working on one of those tricky, sensitive, people problems you never see coming until they land squarely on your plate.

Timely Support To Make Your Job Easier, Can Be Rapidly Found In The HR Inner Circle

As a member of the HR Inner Circle, to get the support you want…

…just ask.

Your first port of call is the vibrant Facebook group, bursting at the seams with incredible HR professionals like you.

Just post your question and let it bubble and simmer in the collective genius of the group.

By the end of the day, you'll have at least 3-5 comments on your post, often more.

You'll get relevant, insightful and practical guidance that comes from the hard earned experience of your fellow members.

Often you'll get a response within a couple of hours. Sometimes you'll get an answer within minutes - even if it's late in the evening!

This highly active community never fails to astound me with just how willing they are to help fellow HR professionals like you.

They readily and generously share their hard earned knowledge and experience.

You Can Get Answers From Real People Quickly AND From Our Extensive Resource Library Too

…really important for someone working on their own who needs to check things out, or just bounce a few ideas around.

- Quentin Colborn
Director, QC People Management Ltd

While you wait for a response from the Facebook group, you'll likely find answers in the resource-rich members' vault on our secure online portal as well.

It takes just 2 clicks and a quick keyword search using our Rapid Results Search Tool.

You'll instantly find precisely where your topic is covered in our extensive back catalogue of monthly magazines and audio seminars.

In under 30 seconds you can find exactly what you're after.

It's that quick and easy.

…And if you need a specific legal insight?

Then pose your question live to an expert employment lawyer in our monthly Q&A session.

It'll either be me or one of my prominent contemporaries. You'll get your answer immediately without having to pay any legal costs.

If you can't wait, you'll find where it's been answered before with a quick search of previous Q&A sessions.

Our clever index system means you can find a question, and in a single click get straight to the recorded answer.

But perhaps you need to dive deep and explore the different options open to you to solve a particularly tricky problem?

Then join one of our monthly HR Huddles. There you can run your specific situation past other HR professionals.

They'll offer their insights, share their experience and work WITH you to find a solution that works FOR you.

You'll find all of this in one convenient place - the HR Inner Circle.

It's Been A Labour Of Love Putting The HR Inner Circle Together So It Works For Professionals Like You

> It's great to see that we all experience tricky cases from time to time.
>
> - Annabelle Carey
> Managing Consultant, HR Services Partnership

I've spent years practising law and have become recognised as one of the UK's leading employment law barristers. I've even got my own radio show!

But more importantly for you, I've also developed another skill.

It's bringing useful employment expertise AND practical experience together in a way that supports busy, overworked (and sometimes stressed) HR professionals like you.

Everything you're likely to need is **literally at your fingertips**.

This will save you time, energy and effort.

Being a member also means your business and clients will see you as even MORE INFORMED about the intricacies of employment law.

They'll marvel at how well you keep up to date when you're busy working so hard for them.

You'll be seen making quicker decisions and implementing effective solutions to accelerate the growth of the organisation.

You'll make impressive time and cost savings for the business.

And those tricky, off-piste situations you've never come across before..?

Well, nothing will faze you, because you're backed up by an HR support system second to none.

But more importantly, you'll feel that pressure gently ease off.

With the relief you'll feel knowing that such great help and guidance is just a few minutes, you'll wonder how you survived without it!

That's Why I'm Inviting You To Join And Reap The Many Rewards Of Membership

▶ WWW.HRINNERCIRCLE.CO.UK ◀

Here's what you get when you join the HR Inner Circle:

Benefit #1- you'll get unlimited access to the hugely popular HR Inner Circle Facebook Private Group

- Tap into the vast wealth of knowledge, experience, insight and wisdom of the top 0.5% of your profession at any time, day or night.

- In less than 5 minutes you can post ANY HR question and get insightful answers and suggestions in a couple of hours or less, from some of the best in your profession.

- Fast track your impact by discovering effective shortcuts and workarounds from HR people who've been "there" and done "it".

- Expand and deepen your network of like minded individuals, secure in the knowledge they're as dedicated and as ambitious as you.

- Increase your prestige with your colleagues and stakeholders by being part of such an exclusive and prominent HR community.

- Gain confidence in your judgment and decisions by using the highly responsive community as a sounding board for your ideas.

Benefit #2 - you'll receive 11 copies of the HR Inner Circular Magazine every year

- Enjoy that satisfying "THUD" on your door mat every month when the postman delivers your very own copy of the HR Inner Circular magazine.

- Quickly discover exactly what the law says about key issues affecting HR professionals around the UK like you.

- Get concise and practical guidance on how employment law applies to the challenging situations and circumstances you deal with every day.

- Avoid the mistakes of others by applying the lessons from the in depth analysis of real life case studies.

- Benefit from a legal deep dive by the UK's leading employment law barrister into a topical employment question posed by a fellow member (perhaps you!).

- Review a summary of recent important Facebook Group discussions worthy of sharing, that you may have missed.

- Explore a range of related and relevant topics useful for your practice and your broader professional development.

> The magazine is really informative, the Facebook group such a community, and I think exceptional value for money.
>
> - Lis Moore
> Head of Advisory & Support Services,
> Society of Local Council Clerks

Benefit #3 - Monthly Audio Seminars

- A 60 minute legal deep dive by me into an important subject relevant to you and your practice.

- Professionally recorded content recorded exclusively for the HR Inner Circle - you'll not find this information anywhere else.

- Carefully structured content that's easy to consume, understand and apply in your work as an HR professional.

- Episodes delivered every month so you can stay current on the latest issues affecting HR professionals.

- The convenience of listening to the recording online or downloading the mp3 for later enjoyment at a time suitable to your busy schedule (perfect for any commute).

Benefit #4 - you get an exclusive invite to a live online Q&A Session every fortnight, led by an expert employment lawyer

- Gain 60 minutes of live and direct access to the sharpest legal minds from my secret little black book of contacts.

- Get answers to your knottiest employment law questions, and solutions to your trickiest HR problems, from some of the brightest employment lawyers in the UK.

- Avoid having to pay the £300-£400 it would cost you to ask a lawyer your question outside of the HR Inner Circle.

- Benefit from valuable insights from the answers given to other members.

- If you can't attend live, watch the recording when it's convenient for you.

- Quickly access the recorded answer to any question asked in the session by simply clicking the question index for that session.

- Save time by downloading the session transcription to scan-read at a time suitable for you.

Benefit #5 - join a live Monthly Huddle with other HR Professionals to solve your most challenging HR problems

- Attend your very own mini-mastermind group of highly qualified, highly regarded and experienced fellow HR professionals to "group think" through an issue you're facing right now.

- Develop bespoke solutions to the unique problems and challenges you have to deal with in a safe, supportive and confidential environment.

- Feel safe knowing these online zoom calls are NOT recorded to respect the sensitivity of issues addressed and the privacy of those involved. [NOTE - a professional transcriber attends and takes written notes. An anonymised summary is then made available to the membership]

- Recent Huddle topics included changing employee benefits, mandatory vaccination, career breaks, sickness during disciplinaries, effective worker forums and hybrid working arrangements.

Benefit #6 - access our Templates & Resources Centre

- Gain immediate access to our library of the most popular and frequently used forms, assessments, agreements, checklists, letter templates, questionnaires and reports to help the busiest HR professionals save time and get things done quicker and easier.

- Download them as Word documents, so you can edit and personalise them to fit your business needs

- New templates added every single month

Benefit #7 - build your own Employment Law Library

- We send you several brand-new books on employment law several times each year

- Acquire your own physical library of concise, easy-to-read and fully updated textbooks

- Recent titles include Hiring Staff, Managing Sickness Absence, Spotting Malingering and Resolving Grievances

Benefit #8 - free Ticket to our Annual Conference

- The perfect opportunity to extend your personal network of fellow HR professionals.

- Meet up face to face with the people who've been supporting you in the Facebook Group and HR Huddles so you can deepen those connections even further.

- Gather key insights and takeaways to help you personally and professionally from some of the best speakers on the circuit. Previous speakers have covered motivation, dealing with difficult people, goal setting and productivity, decision making and social media marketing.

- Get instant access to recordings of all previous conferences so even if you can't attend in person, you can benefit from the event in your own time.

- Includes probably the best conference lunch you'll ever have - a bold claim I know, but we use outstanding caterers.

> It never ceases to amaze me the amount of time and effort people put into the Facebook group, sharing their experiences, advice, and sage words of wisdom.
>
> - Emma Lister
> HR Consultant, SME HR Services

Benefit #9 - your Personal Concierge will help you get the best out of your membership

- You get personal access to Nina who'll point you in the direction of exactly where to find what you need. She's supported hundreds of members over the 5 years she's been part of the team.

- Nina also works closely with the 11 back office staff that support the operation. In the extremely unlikely event she doesn't know where something is, she knows who will.

HOW MUCH DOES JOINING THE HR INNER CIRCLE COST?

There's no doubt in my mind the annual value of membership benefits is in the many thousands of pounds range.

But you're not going to pay anywhere near that.

Let me remind you of what that small monthly fee gives you every year

Access to the private Facebook Group	INCLUDED
HR Inner Circular Magazine subscription	INCLUDED
Monthly Audio Seminars	INCLUDED
Live Q&A sessions	INCLUDED
Monthly HR Huddles	INCLUDED
Templates & Resources Centre	INCLUDED
Employment Law Library	INCLUDED
Free ticket to the HR Inner Circle Annual Conference	INCLUDED
Your Personal Membership Concierge	INCLUDED

TOTAL PRICELESS

Another way of looking at your investment is this:

Because access to what you need is so quick…

Join today and that price is fixed for as long as you remain a member.   You'll always pay the same, even if we increase the price to new members (which we regularly do).

…it's like having your very own part time, legally trained, assistant HR Business Partner, just waiting to provide you with all the answers you need…

▶ WWW.HRINNERCIRCLE.CO.UK ◀

Plus, With Membership Of The HR Inner Circle, You'll Also Get These 4 Additional Resources For FREE!

Additional Resource #1 - Handling Awkward Conversations

A video case study masterclass you can share with managers to train them to handle awkward staff disciplinary, performance and attitude problems. A huge time saver for you.

Additional Resource #2 - 6 x HR Employment Online Courses

Immediate, on demand access to six thorough, online HR courses (with more constantly added), including Employment Tribunal Compensation, Chat GPT for HR Professionals, Deconstructing TUPE, Changing Terms & Conditions, Unconscious Bias At Work and Handling Grievances.

Additional Resource #3 - Free listing on the Register of Investigators

Advertise your professional investigations service in our member's portal.

Additional Resource #4 - Significant discounts on sets of policies, contracts, and other courses.

Get member discounts on my Getting Redundancy Right and HR Policies products as well as other price reductions as new products are released.

WWW.HRINNERCIRCLE.CO.UK

> It's a really good investment. The support you get from other Facebook group members is fantastic. Whatever your question, someone will know the answer. Access to Daniel's experience and knowledge through the podcasts and Q&A is invaluable too.
>
> - Tracy Madgwick
> HR Consultant, Crafnant HR

I'm So Confident Joining The HR Inner Circle Is The Right Decision For You, Here's My

NO LIMITS

GUARANTEE

Take action and join the HR Inner Circle **now**.

If you're not 100% satisfied with your investment, you can cancel at ANY time.

Just tell us, and your membership will end immediately. No long-term contracts. No notice periods. No fuss.

I'm comfortable doing this because I know once you join, you'll find the support, the information and the strategies so useful, you'll never want to leave.

Before you decide though, let me be very clear about membership of the HR Inner Circle.

It's only for ambitious and dedicated HR professionals who want to accelerate and increase their impact by plugging into an HR ecosystem with its finger firmly on the pulse of what's working right now in HR.

If you're just plodding along and are content with just getting by, then this is probably not for you.

But if you're drawn to benefiting from standing shoulder to shoulder with some of the giants in the HR community who will help you solve your toughest problems, then joining the HR Inner Circle is the RIGHT decision for you.

Join here now:

▶ WWW.HRINNERCIRCLE.CO.UK ◀

JOIN TODAY

Daniel Barnett

P.S. Remember when you join you get unrestricted access to the private Facebook group, the monthly magazine delivered direct to your door, the monthly audio seminar, regular free books, templates, checklists and resources, on-demand video courses, over 100 audio seminars and back copies of magazines, live interactive Q&A sessions with a lawyer, focused monthly huddles with other HR professionals, a free ticket to the annual conference, your personal concierge plus a bunch of additional resources…